The Campus History Series

WATERFORD
COUNTRY SCHOOL
1922–2022

Waterford Country School's circle of children and staff has endured through time and to this day embodies the concept of strength through community spirit and togetherness. This Waterford Country School (WCS) logo is used today as a graphic representation of its revered past and serves as a reminder of how the soul heals by being surrounded by those who understand and care. (Courtesy of Waterford Country School Inc.)

ON THE COVER: From its inception, Waterford Country School pledged its dedication to doing whatever it takes to enrich the lives of youth and strengthen families through specialized program resources and community services. The circle of children and staff holding hands in unity is how each day started and ended, then and now. Its symbolism is clear: children and teenagers will never be alone, and someone will always be there and ready to catch them if they fall. (Courtesy of Waterford Country School Inc.)

COVER BACKGROUND: The architects of Waterford Country School strongly believed that the bond created between student and animal is indelible and will last a lifetime. The farm animals are a vital part of the curriculum and cannot be overemphasized. Students are outside every day watching them and caring for them. Teachers maintain that having animals at the forefront of the curriculum enables students to observe and interact at the farm and then return to the classroom where they can expand on what they have seen through personal accounts, play, or research. Students often get totally engaged in watching or interacting with an animal and the episodes become a positive feature of the day, often providing an effective way to transition from an unsettled moment. (Courtesy of Waterford Country School Inc.)

The Campus History Series

WATERFORD COUNTRY SCHOOL
1922–2022

BENJAMIN S. TURNER

FOREWORD BY WILLIAM MARTIN

ARCADIA PUBLISHING

Copyright © 2022 by Benjamin S. Turner
ISBN 978-1-4671-0859-1

Published by Arcadia Publishing
Charleston, South Carolina

Printed in the United States of America

Library of Congress Control Number: 2022934083

For all general information, please contact Arcadia Publishing:
Telephone 843-853-2070
Fax 843-853-0044
E-mail sales@arcadiapublishing.com
For customer service and orders:
Toll-Free 1-888-313-2665

Visit us on the Internet at www.arcadiapublishing.com

*To all those who made, and continue to make,
Waterford Country School a village brimming
with hope, healing, and strength.*

CONTENTS

FOREWORD

I met Ettie Schacht, our surviving Waterford Country School founder, in the fall of 1979. I was a 24-year-old new staff member at the school, and she was in her 90s, sitting in her wheelchair on the campus lawn and watching the children run around. Little did I know at the time that this meeting with the founder of the school would lead me to become the executive director, serving until the 98th year of the school.

My 41-year journey at Waterford Country School was not by any means easy but became the greatest experience of my professional life. I never planned to spend my entire career there, but never once thought of leaving. I found a deep sense of purpose at Waterford Country School, but more importantly, found an exceptional group of others who would join the journey, share the purpose, and stay with the school for much of their professional lives. These were the right people, staying for the right reasons, and we built a team of staff and board members second to none. As we "inherited" the family business, we realized that we were developing a family business of unrelated people.

Before we knew it, our staff and board tenure were averaging 19 years of service. This was an incredible feat in our profession and became the core of our strength to help our troubled youth. We all shared the awareness that the behaviors of the young people were a manifestation of symptoms that came from a source of pain. We needed to develop strong relationships with the youth to provide a secure base for them to begin to address their past trauma. We knew that treating the symptoms would not heal the wounds, but treating the wounds would relieve the symptoms. We also learned to treat each other with the same principles of care and compassion.

In the four decades of my time at WCS, our amazing group of staff developed many new programs, built state-of-the-art facilities, and helped thousands of children change the trajectory of their lives from hopelessness and despair to a positive outlook and happiness. The active ingredient was the connection between the staff members and the young people and that became the conduit for change and hope.

We are forever grateful for the privilege of having stepped into children's lives at a very dark time and being a part of their growth and positive change. That's who we were, who we are, and who we will be going forward in the next 100 years.

—William Martin, MHSA
Executive Director, Retired
Fall 2021

ACKNOWLEDGMENTS

Writing this book and capturing a century of achievement proved to be a challenging task. As the new guy on the block, having served only 12 years compared to those who have served WCS for decades, I was prompted to ask for help, and a number of people stepped forward and offered their assistance. Some shared stories, others offered advice, and still, others directed me to books and documents about this amazing school of ours. I need to say at the outset that I am not a professional writer nor a historian, and I am not ashamed to admit that I was totally overwhelmed when I first saw the massive accumulation of newspaper clippings, photographs, scrapbooks, school programs, letters, postcards, plaques, diaries, artistic sketches, and assorted blueprints amassed over 100 years. I asked myself if I had the willpower, energy, and time to make sense of that overwhelming stockpile of historical artifacts, praying that critics would go easy on me and not hang me out to dry.

Unless otherwise noted, all images in this publication appear courtesy of Waterford Country School Inc. and its photograph and public relations archives. This project could not have been possible without the inspiration, collaboration, and support of Dr. Jeff Turner. I wish to extend special gratitude to Elena French, Dr. Julianna Velazquez, and Jessica Michon for shepherding a large assortment of photographs and documents from the forefront my way, all of which helped me to better understand and chart the school's heritage and growth over the past 100 years. Chief executive officer Chris Lacey provided an unending flow of supportive guidance and advice. William Martin, executive emeritus director, shed informative and nostalgic memories with history in mind, and his insights helped me to further navigate WCS's historic trail. Gregg Turner and Casey Turner inspired enthusiasm down in Florida to get the project started with Arcadia Publishing. Arcadia Publishing's staff Caitrin Cunningham and Jeff Ruetsche gave our team hope to uncover this hidden gem.

I also send along my appreciation to a village of supporters who supplied assistance and unwavering support as my manuscript evolved and eventually acquired its final shape. In particular, I wish to thank Anne Adams, Dr. Bruce and Kathy Saunders, Chris Howe, Christine Hammond, Dave Moorehead, Eileen Degaetano, Emily Schacht, Dr. Gene Shultze, Guy Scribner, Gordon and Ramona Ramsay, Julianna Wasniewski, Kelly Walker, Kimberly Paradise, Lorri Saunders, Nancy Turner, Pamela Giannelli, Pamela Schacht, Dr. Ray Johnson, Rick and Pam McPherson, Robert "Chip" Anderson, Robert and Teresa Schacht, Sharon Butcher, Ted and Eileen Olynciw, Tina Cote, Dr. Thomas and Reta Schacht. In addition, I would like to thank the WCS Board of Trustees, Expanded Leadership Team, Camp Cuheca, and the founding family.

It is worthy to note that the publishing guidelines for this book dictated a strict format. The number of photographs, the number of words in a caption, and the number of pages in the book were predetermined and left no room for negotiation. This meant I could not include everything, be it people, programs, events, facilities, and the like.

Finally, it is my team's hope that they created a truly unique book, one that you will want to keep on your bookshelf knowing that you will take it down someday and want to read it again. In the end, I hope you will find this book enjoyable and enlightening, and that the result will be greater appreciation and understanding of Waterford Country School's rich and storied history. It has been an honor for me to write this book.

INTRODUCTION

One hundred years ago, we did not know much about how a child's mind worked, let alone how adversity and maladjustment impacted the course of growth and development. For the most part, maladaptive behavior among children and youth was talked about little in bygone eras. An overriding theme was that children were expected to be seen but not heard, especially the maladjusted.

Youthful dysfunctional behaviors were often seen as moral issues, thus deserving of reprimand or even punishment. Childhood and youth disturbances did not have their own category within the mental illness spectrum; consequently, there were no disorders specific to youngsters. Those children afflicted with behavioral disorders were often kept away from the neighborhood mainstream and were likely to create parental shame, embarrassment, and guilt. The same held true for children born with mental disabilities.

More than a few youngsters exhibiting psychological maladjustment or found to be guilty of delinquent or incorrigible behavior were sent away to houses of refuge, congregate institutions that were often overcrowded and deteriorating. Many of the wayward were confined there simply because there were no other options. While such arrangements were supposedly designed to help the deviant, the truth of the matter was that these placements offered little support, guidance, and avenues for recovery. Staff abuse and neglect were not uncommon occurrences. Many staff members were untrained and indifferent to the needs of the special population, prompting some observers to remark that it was the helpers who needed the help, not the children.

Our houses of refuge and other shelters such as reformatories or institutional care for the mentally deficient were the solution for removing challenged youngsters from the view of both the family and community. For many parents, such locations were for unruly, troubled youngsters, or those labeled "feeble-minded," thus relieving guardian keepers from childrearing responsibilities. Once committed, troubled, or "backward," children rarely saw their families again.

But as the century wore on, our perceptions of children and youth began to change, and an entire discipline dedicated to the scientific study of younger generations moved to the forefront. Children were seen as morphing from dependent and helpless youngsters to individuals needing schooling and less punitive parental measures. But this did not mean that attitudes changed overnight. Those labeled as "troubled" or "different" were still viewed with concern and suspicion, not only in the home but also in the school and surrounding community.

Social reformers in the early 1920s urged a greater emphasis on educational intervention. Their efforts resulted in a surge of training and industrial schools, along with a number of new innovations including cottage residential institutions, out-of-home placements, and parent education programs. Child guidance clinics also came to the forefront around this time, adding to our growing understanding of the multiple factors involved in the development of childhood disorders. Child guidance clinics sprung up and sought to offer proactive approaches designed to promote children's health and mental well-being, rather than relying solely on reactionary measures.

Also appearing at this time were a number of nationwide efforts to improve the quality of the school experience for the special needs child, including the creation of new educational alternatives. Regarding the latter, one of the more prominent breakthroughs was Connecticut's Waterford Country School. The 100-year evolution of this landmark institution rests at the foundation of this book and readers will be taken on an engaging visual voyage, one that traces the school's modest and humble beginnings to its present-day national status.

The school began in 1922 on a small scale in the home of Ettie and Henry Schacht, two New York public school teachers. After having three children, Ettie left her teaching position to stay home and care for her children, two of whom were sickly. But she did not give up her love for teaching; rather, she and Henry established a day school in their Brooklyn home for young children. While Ettie was the teaching mainstay, Henry continued working in the public-school sector to support the family, as well as using his theatrical background to act in a number of Hollywood, Broadway, and stock theater productions.

The Schacht home school was an immediate success, due mostly to Ettie's extraordinary talents as a teacher, advocate, and mentor. News of the home school spread fast. The popularity of it rested on the shoulders of Ettie, particularly her ability to teach the child with special needs. She worked alongside children who were gifted as well as those having mental deficiencies. She taught the blind as well as those afflicted with polio or other physical impairments. She taught the emotionally abused in addition to handicapped immigrant children who couldn't speak English. To reach such a diverse population, she had to create innovative and unorthodox pedagogy. In short, her teaching techniques and methods worked. Suffice it to say that Ettie Schacht believed in "mainstreaming" long before it became an accepted practice in today's school systems.

But her many successes in the Schacht home school came with a price. Despite the fact that Ettie's skills were lauded by educational admirers, folks nearby were indifferent and baffled—if not hostile—toward the new home school springing up in their neighborhood. Many felt that the children with special needs were contagious or dangerous and needed to be relocated far away from their locale. The neighbors cringed when they saw severely handicapped or physically disfigured children getting out of vehicles and disappearing into the Schacht household. The children were met with wide-eyed stares, especially those who hobbled with assistance from a guardian or those who relied on a cane or wheelchair. They watched as Ettie warmly greeted the youngsters each day and welcomed them into her home.

The neighbors were beside themselves. They tried to close the doors of the school on numerous occasions, making numerous complaints to housing authorities. In the first year of operation, the Schachts were taken to court 17 times. Ettie stood up for her rights each time and convinced the court that the work she was doing benefitted not only her pupils but also their parents and society as a whole. She won every court hearing.

In 1925, as the number of incoming students swelled and exceeded physical space, Ettie and Henry realized they needed to find a larger physical setting. In that year they leased an estate in Far Rockaway, New York, as a summer camp, then in 1926 purchased two buildings in Brooklyn, a facility they named the Buckingham School. The latter had an occupancy for 60 children, and because it was certified as a boarding school, many of the children were present 24 hours a day, seven days a week, instead of just during regular school hours. The school population was racially and religiously diverse, and many of the children were visibly handicapped.

Similar to earlier times, a neighborhood fray erupted, originating from a mixture of intolerance and ignorance, which in turn bred fear and even superstition. The neighbors called upon regulatory and licensing agencies to shut the school down, but the school passed each inspection with flying colors. But while the neighbors did not succeed in closing the school, they did find a technicality that created a problem. The certificate of occupancy specified that the main building was zoned for a boarding home, not a school. While the youngsters could legally sleep, eat, and play inside the building, they could not be educated inside it.

But a stroke of genius by the Schachts enabled them to sidestep the zoning infraction and keep the school intact. Quite simply, they chose to conduct their classes outdoors, similar to the open-air schools operating at the time in Switzerland. The Schacht school was held outside in good weather and on covered porches during inclement weather, all year long. The benefits of an open-air format were ahead of its time back in the day, and in these modern times is recognized as a means to help prevent the spread of COVID-19 and its variants as well as other infectious diseases.

In 1929, fueled by their successes but unable to accommodate the growing demand for their services, the Schachts searched for property having suitable expansive possibilities. They found the property of their dreams in Waterford, Connecticut, a 500-acre tract of property offering rich soil and beautiful farmlands, sweeping hay fields, and a picturesque stream of fresh water emptying into a placid, beautiful lake. The Schachts purchased the property with the vision of outdoor education in mind along with a proven track record of understanding and meeting the needs of children with special needs. With the property deed in hand, the seeds of Waterford Country School were sown.

Waterford Country School would go on and establish its roots in this bucolic setting, in the process establishing itself as a haven for troubled children and teenagers, a waystation for those suffering from hurt and disability. Most of the afflicted suffered from neglect and multiple impairments. They looked to the Waterford Country School as a place for recovery, a retreat offering hope and a gateway for a better, happier, and meaningful life.

How did Waterford Country School achieve such remarkable standards of hope and recovery? What kinds of care did the school render that would make their clients more adaptable to whatever their later lives might present? How did it manage to integrate outdoor education into its academic curriculum? Such questions are best answered by opening the school's one-hundred-year-old time capsule and peering inside. Why not climb aboard and take a look? You will be surprised at what you will find—most of all, a story begging to be told.

One
HUMBLE BEGINNINGS

The historical roots of
Waterford Country School
were not tucked away in
the tranquil countryside
of Waterford, Connecticut.
Rather, founders Henry
and Ettie Schacht founded
a school of their own in
1922, then established
the Buckingham Street
School in 1926. Because of
zoning restrictions, classes
could only be conducted
outside the buildings on
Buckingham Street. In
this photograph, tykes
and tots cheer on a turtle
race. Note the children's
winter clothing, and in the
background, a chalkboard
and teacher's desk.

This Schacht family portrait captures (clockwise from top center) Rita, Ettie, Herb, Henry, and Babette. The Schacht family would become pioneers in the development of Waterford Country School. They will long be remembered for groundbreaking accomplishments in the field of special education, especially their steadfast determination to nurture and promote the motto, "Where Everybody Is Somebody." To deliver on this motto, the Schacht family had to transform a farm nestled in the woodlands of Connecticut into a school offering individualized attention in the classroom along with a curriculum embracing outdoor education. The school has lost none of its luster over the years and withstood the test of time, in the process becoming a highly successful and prominent learning institution.

Ettie Thomas Schacht immigrated from Russia and quickly developed a reputation as a gifted teacher, someone who had a knack for teaching stubborn and obstinate pupils. Her supervisors made note of her patience and calmness in the classroom, most notably her skill for connecting with even the hardest to reach pupils. Her teaching dedication was superior. She launched her teaching career at an early age in the New York City Public School System and immigrant students flocked to her classes. She was recognized as a tireless and devoted educator, someone who would go to great lengths to see her students excel in their studies.

Henry Schacht also immigrated from Russia and graduated from Cornell University in 1908, majoring in dramatic arts and education. He joined the New York Public School System, teaching languages and physical education. It was here that he met Ettie Schacht, and after a relatively short courtship, they married in 1913. The couple had three children, Rita, Babette, and Herb. While Ettie stayed home to care for Babette and Herb, Henry continued teaching to support his family.

While Ettie Schacht remained at home to care for her children, she did not let her interest in childhood development evaporate. Instead, she created a home school in their residence on Union Street in Brooklyn, New York, in 1922. She dubbed her program the "Culture and Health School," and she utilized her special education skills to provide structured, tender instruction, and guidance. In those days, since there were no publicly supported programs for handicapped youngsters, Ettie's home school was an overnight success.

Employing pioneering vision and creative teaching methods, Ettie provided children with relaxed, free-play activities encouraging cooperation and compliance. Ettie hired a staff of teachers and trained them in her methods, resulting in a program providing an unending supply of acceptance, understanding, and love. Ettie and her staff provided a climate of life filled with opportunities for children to change and grow. Ettie helped her children find confidence in their abilities and the inner strength to overcome adversity. These early educational experiences eventually helped the youngsters to see concrete hope for a brighter, happier life.

The Union Street home school continued to gain in popularity, but in the process created a sizable waiting list. In 1926, Henry and Ettie Schacht realized they needed to expand their programming and moved into a facility named "the Buckingham School" after the road in Brooklyn where it was located. The school consisted of two buildings next to one another and was zoned as a boarding school for 60 children. Meanwhile, the Union Street home school remained open and, for a few years, was supervised by Ettie's mother, Rose Thomas.

There would be an interesting twist to the Schachts' relocation. Most of the residents of Buckingham Road wanted no part of a school encroaching upon their neighborhood and called upon various regulatory and licensing agencies to prevent it from happening. Building departments, health departments, and fire departments found no fault with the premises. However, the certificate of occupancy was for a boarding home, not a school. But the Schachts were not to be deterred. They got around this technicality by conducting classes outside in good weather, and under roofed porches during inclement weather, all year long. Such settings were modeled after the open-air classes of Switzerland and provided the health benefits of clean, fresh air. The image above captured one of the ingenious outdoor seating arrangements fashioned by the Schachts for a teacher and students. Below, children are dressed for cold weather instruction.

As word spread about the successes of the Union Street and Buckingham Road schools, the Schachts decided to purchase a bus for those children in need of transportation. The bus was also used for field trips and other excursions, including to Far Rockaway during the summer months. Because the heat was often unbearable at both schools during the summer months, a leased summer estate in Far Rockaway offered spacious grounds, a swimming pool, and an estate that sat near the ocean. The camp was large enough to accommodate all the children and staff. Families were also encouraged to stop by and visit the summer accommodations. The school's bus appears in the background of the image above, while the below photograph captures campers cooling off on a hot New York summer day.

An important feature of the Culture and Health School's offerings was the emphasis placed on such activities as singing, dancing, role-playing, artistic creation, storytelling, and other performing arts. Henry Schacht masterminded this facet of the curriculum and was proud of the impact it had on the children. Henry worked in the theater industry and was a noted professional character actor on the New York stage, going under the name Henry Sharp. It was Henry's acting income which to a large extent supported the creation of the Brooklyn schools and later the acquisition of the Connecticut property. Henry can be seen in the image above (far left foreground) of a theater troupe, as parents mingle with child actors and actresses. Below, a theater production is conducted on a makeshift stage nestled between the two Buckingham School buildings.

Buoyed by their educational successes in Brooklyn, Henry and Ettie Schacht set their sights on acquiring a rural setting, one enabling them to escape from their cramped New York quarters and offering wide expansive possibilities. In 1929, they found such a setting in Waterford, Connecticut. Named the Josephson Farm, the property consisted of 650 acres, two very large, old farmhouses, a dairy barn, a stream called Hunt's Brook, and a large lake (see below). The property was purchased by the Schachts in addition to Ettie's sister Dora and her husband, William (Henry's brother), who gave their house in Flushing, Long Island, as a down payment. It was an investment no one would ever regret or forget.

The Schachts spent five days exploring the Josephson property before making the purchase. They marveled at what they called "enchanting country." They loved the peacefulness of the surrounding woods, its tranquility enhanced by the absence of manmade noise. Almost immediately they felt a calm connection to nature. They hiked over rustic bridges, through wooded areas, out into large fields of soft, undulating country, the fragrance of wildflowers following them everywhere. They spent time at the lake, resting in the shade of cliffs overhanging the lake's border. Almost always they came upon the soft, murmuring brook, upon whose edges of soft green carpet paths enticed them. They spent countless hours imagining the use of farmland, terrain, natural resources, use of existing structures, and placement of service buildings to create a climate of life-learning experiences to best meet the special needs of challenged children and youth.

The Josephson dairy barn and its surroundings in 1929 offer a sharp contrast to the goings-on of the Experiential Education Center today. While the dairy barn still stands, the landscape has been transformed by the Children's Farm and Nature Center, an animal sanctuary, a state and federally licensed Wildlife Rehabilitation Center, horse stable and corrals, an adventure ropes course, and an animal-assisted therapy/activities venue.

The Schachts possessed the vision to regard the 1929 dairy barn as a valuable means to provide older students with unique on-the-job training, opportunities that could instill confidence and a sense of achievement. Under close supervision, they envisioned students working alone or in groups depending on the duties assigned. Such duties might include feeding and watering calves, sweeping and washing the milking area, washing the milking equipment, or feeding and bedding the cows.

Dirt roads were often bordered by rocks painted white that helped guide visitors and campers to various destinations. This particular location in 1930 was designed as a picnic area and respite from the summer sun. Note the circular bench around the tree in the left foreground and the shelter in the background, the latter serving as public toilets and washrooms. Today, this area no longer exists and has been replaced by Founders Park, dedicated in 2021.

Transportation of children and staff to and from camp locations often consisted of riding in horse-drawn hay wagons such as the one pictured here. Hay trucks were also used for various purposes. For example, when the camp first opened, 60 children traveled by ferry from New York City to New London, Connecticut. At the dock, they boarded hay trucks that brought them from the New London pier to the Waterford camp.

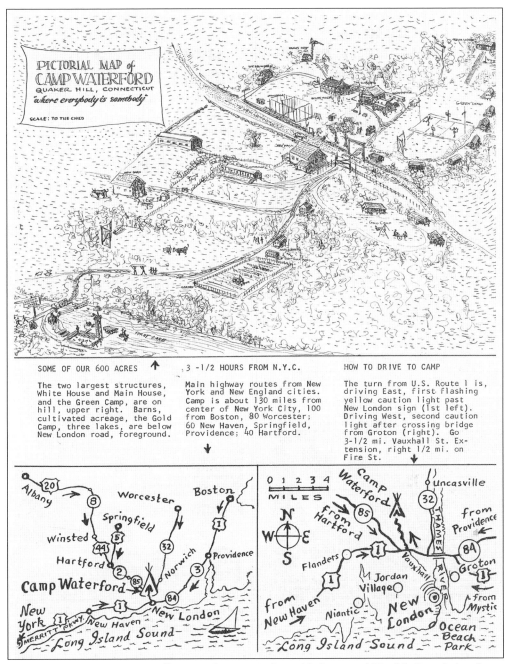

PICTORIAL MAP of CAMP WATERFORD
QUAKER HILL, CONNECTICUT
"where everybody is somebody"

SCALE: TO THE CHILD

SOME OF OUR 600 ACRES ↑

The two largest structures, White House and Main House, and the Green Camp, are on hill, upper right. Barns, cultivated acreage, the Gold Camp, three lakes, are below New London road, foreground.

, 3 -1/2 HOURS FROM N.Y.C.

Main highway routes from New York and New England cities. Camp is about 130 miles from center of New York City, 100 from Boston, 80 Worcester; 60 New Haven, Springfield, Providence; 40 Hartford.

↓

HOW TO DRIVE TO CAMP

The turn from U.S. Route 1 is, driving East, first flashing yellow caution light past New London sign (1st left). Driving West, second caution light after crossing bridge from Groton (right). Go 3-1/2 mi. Vauxhall St. Extension, right 1/2 mi. on Fire St. ↓

The summer camp was initially named Camp Cuheca (Culture and Health Camp), but later, its name was changed to Camp Waterford. Camp life in the early going was both rustic and oftentimes makeshift. Most of the children and staff slept in Army tents. Drinking water came from a hand pump on a dug well. The toilets were primitive. Electricity was supplied by a Delco generator and battery system that supplied 32 volts when it worked. Cooking was done on a wood and coal stove. But the Schachts were visionaries and saw great promise for the camp. This c. 1957 sketch depicts future development possibilities.

In time, improvements found their way to the summer camp. Bungalows with porches such as those captured above and below were constructed for boys and girls and were equipped with sanitary washrooms. An outside dining hall of rustic cedar was constructed to complement the indoor facility. As far as camp activities were concerned, Ettie Schacht believed that learning was best accomplished around real-life experiences. Young campers enjoyed playtime, sports and games, campfires, singing, dancing, hayrides, swimming, and hiking. Developmentally appropriate chores were also assigned, such as cleaning, helping to cook, growing food on the farm, or blocking up the nearby brook to create a swimming hole. Arts and crafts as well as bus trips to destinations such as museums, parks, or public beaches were among children's favorites.

For older children and teenagers, various games and sports were offered at Camp Waterford. Here on the main athletic field in 1934, teens had access to the creation of a baseball diamond (above). Note the position of the backstop and the three bungalows once again in the background. Games promoted a healthy rivalry between the older campers. Below, the main athletic field was converted into tennis courts with simple alterations made to the enclosures. Rivalries from the spring carried over to the fall, the competition sparking team cohesiveness and togetherness. Camp counselors served as coaches and encouraged the players to abide by the spirit of fellowship and goodwill.

Basketball was another favorite among the older teenagers. Given the school's limited expenses, a homemade basketball court was designed, the dimensions occupying a grass strip outside the camp bungalows. The backboards consisted of planking and the makeshift rims hardly qualified as regulation height. No nets hung from the rims, and the goalposts, cut and stripped from the nearby forest, supported the backboards. The substitute court features did not matter to the players. They played hard, serving notice that the spirit of pickup basketball was alive and well in the 1930s. Indeed, the competition between rival teams was fierce. In the image below, a camp counselor (left, white shirt) referees a match between two opponents playing on the grass surface.

Art classes were among the most popular activities at Camp Waterford, largely because of the scenic beauty surrounding the premises. Birds swoop by, butterflies flutter about, and squirrels rustle in the trees. Campers seek to create such images of nature by using a variety of artistic techniques, such as charcoal sketching, acrylic paint, watercolor, oil and chalk pastel, and colored pencils. Camp Waterford supplies its nature trails and creative spark while children's imaginations do the rest. Plus, there are bonuses beyond the finished piece. Of course, art increases creativity and imagination. But art also enhances fine motor skills, hand-eye coordination, problem-solving skills, lateral thinking, complex analysis, and critical-thinking skills. Art also enables children to learn from their mistakes and be open to the realm of other possibilities. The support of fellow campers and an encouraging instructor can be the push that a youngster needs to engage in artistic creation.

In the 1930s, the first day of May was celebrated at WCS by watching dancers weave ribbons around a maypole, in this case, the tall flagpole at the center of the campus. Activities such as dancing and gymnastics were held underneath. The maypole tradition dates back centuries long ago. The maypole and its ribbons represented symbols of the shift from the dreary and raw cold season to the livelier warmer one. The maypole at WCS was designed to embrace unity, wholeness, and community and became an annual spring celebration, providing a centerpiece for students to dance and spread happiness.

One of the many trademarks of Camp Waterford was the emphasis placed on theater and dance, a tradition first launched by the Culture and Health School. For young children, it was believed that dance and creative movement can help enhance creativity, cognitive skills, and social development. It also provides opportunities to exercise both gross and fine motor skills. From turning and jumping to achieving balance and timing, dance engages many aspects of a child's physical development. In the image above, angels are rehearsing a play (note the wire wings each angel is wearing), while the below photograph captures children synchronizing a dance routine. Later, both groups of youngsters will showcase their talents on stage before the entire camp.

Campers were attracted to the nearby lakes fed by the waters of Hunts Brook. During the early camp years, children delighted in water activities (above). The lake in particular presented opportunities for wading, fishing, and boating opportunities. In years to come, water activities would expand and offer children and adolescents a wide array of recreational activities. It might be added that the territory surrounding the three-mile lake offered a rich terrain for hiking and exploration. Following swimming and boating activities, campers dried off and soaked up the sun on lounge chairs (below), many of which were crafted by older children in carpentry classes.

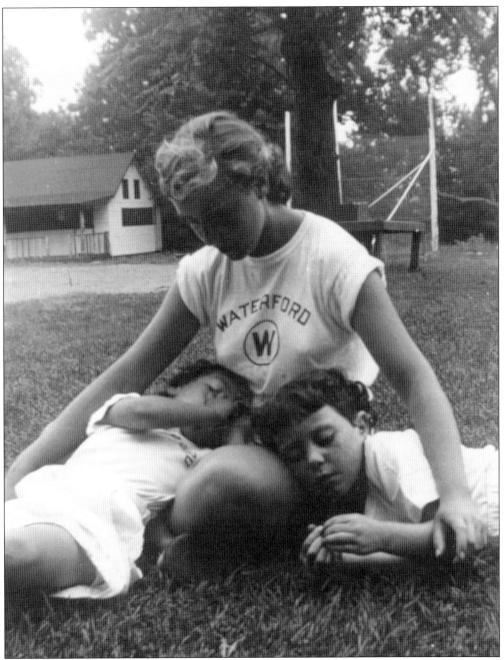

Of course, some of the younger campers needed more attention and tender care. Camp counselors were trained in ways to enhance children's comfort, positivity, and security. Obviously, these two tykes felt secure enough to seek comfort and find peace of mind from this female counselor. Whether it be indoor or outdoor activities, camp supervisors expected its counselors to always come across as caring, calm, and well-adjusted people, never cold or detached. The supervisors believed that a child feels secure when bonding happens, particularly when it is done consistently. The end result is trust between the camper and the counselor.

In 1939, Babette Schacht, Ettie and Henry's middle child, passed away at the age of 20. Babette is pictured in the photograph above with her maternal grandmother, Rose Thomas. Babette developed rheumatic heart disease as a child and had difficulty her entire life with tasks requiring physical exertion. Inspired by her sister Rita, she wanted to become an artist and attended school in Colorado to achieve her lifelong dreams. While there, she contracted strep throat, and because no antibiotics existed at the time, the infection spread into her already weakened heart and took her life. She was the first of her family to be buried in the Cuheca Cemetery, located next to the historic Ames and Bolles Cemetery in Waterford. Pictured left is Babette's gravestone and memorial.

The tragic loss of Babette was devastating for Ettie. She was overwhelmed with grief and mourning. Her creative spirit fell victim to heartbreak and remorse. She confessed to those around her that her energies for Camp Waterford were depleted, as well as her mounting duties and obligations, prompting her to return home to New York where she imparted guidance and advice to the Waterford school. These photographs capture Ettie's charisma and charm just before she departed from Waterford: escorting a young lad to camp activities (above) and speaking to campers (below). She left Camp Waterford shortly after these photographs were taken.

The sudden departure of Ettie from Camp Waterford created concern as well as uncertainty about the camp's future. However, it also presented an opportunity for improvement and upgrades to the school property. The idea of creating a year-round camp in Waterford had been bandied back and forth for some time. The concept had always been a dream but now with the grounds empty, a plan was put into action. Beginning in 1940, workers began to winterize the summer camp bungalows (above). Also, dilapidated and unused buildings (below) were leveled so that new structures could be built and easily accessed.

A building that withstood the test of time for many years was Cedar Lodge, a multipurpose structure once located behind the current Anderson House. Cedar Lodge offered easy access to both students and staff and became a landmark of sorts for the WCS campus. Much of this was due to its architecture. At a distance, the structure resembled a chalet or alpine design with its peaked roof and sloped roofline, a staggered and steeped stairway, and a decorative and ornamental frontal porch and railing. According to past staffers, it had a "hide-a-way" appearance. The interior design offered knotty pine walls, a beamed ceiling, wide-planked floors, a cedar-shingled exterior, and a foundation partly resting on a boulder foundation. Cedar Lodge served many school functions over the course of its lifespan, including as a lodging, meeting place, classroom, offices, and visitation center, among others.

The White House (above) was one of the oldest structures on the grounds and required the most attention. The walls of the entire structure needed to be insulated, the roof replaced, and a coal-and-wood-fired boiler installed along with piping and radiators to provide heat. Interior plumbing needed to be winterized, and all the interior rooms and the building's exterior needed a fresh coat of paint. Eventually, the White House became a dormitory, accommodating 20 boys on the first floor and 18 boys on the second floor. A small apartment was located on the third floor for the resident director. The photograph below captures a refurbished look at the improved bungalows and the landscaped summer campgrounds.

The decision to create a year-round camp required a reorganization of leadership. As renovation at the empty camp began in 1940, Ettie and Henry decided to remain home in New York and orchestrate changes from afar. They appointed their daughter Rita and her husband, Bo Saunders, to head the Buckingham School in New York, which now ran only a day program. Additionally, Rita and Bo were assigned to direct the summer program in Waterford when the camp reopened. Here, the new pre-vocational car program is showcased by Rita's son, Gary (above), while on another occasion, she confers with her mother, Ettie (below).

Bo and Rita had two sons, Gary and Bruce. Bo Saunders (above, second row, far right) was no stranger to Camp Waterford, and his presence was felt in many different ways. Bo had been a pilot during World War II, and among other assignments transported combat supplies to American troops and our allies. Bo was recalled to active duty to serve in the Korean War in 1951 and never returned to the Waterford camp or school. Bo's sons followed in their father's footsteps and became pilots. In later years, Bruce became the clinical and educational director at Waterford Country School and president of the board of trustees (from 1972 to 1976) before moving to Bangor, Maine, and starting his own private practice. In the left image, Bruce (left) delivers a speech at the school alongside Tom Schacht, the latter having worked in the development department at WCS and later became yet another prominent psychologist.

Pictured right, Gary Saunders founded Coastal Air Services at the Groton-New London Airport in 1976. Coastal Air Services grew from a single location to a five-location regional charter operator and aircraft sales business. Below, even in these modern times, the Saunders' home on campus is simply called "Rita's House" in her memory. Following her passing in 1974, Rita's House became a transitional unit for youngsters who were closest to discharge, and able to function productively in public school and in the community. It later became the location for WCS's Spiritual Life Program, under the leadership of Susan Sullivan, RN, director of medical services. As a multifaceted, vintage building on campus, Rita's House served many WCS programs over the years, including the high school, life skills classes, and clinical offices under the leadership of Principal Sharon Butcher.

In 1942, after a two-year absence, the year-round and newly named "Cuheca Country School" opened its doors to children with special needs. Renovations and repairs were still underway but did not deter enrollment or stem community interest. Ettie and Henry Schacht remained in New York overseeing the school's operation. The downside of the early years and a prickly thorn was finding the right director to manage the Waterford school. Three school directors came and left over the next four years. The reasons for their departure were multiple: the conditions were too primitive, the demands of maintaining old buildings and a working farm too overwhelming, and the children's needs were endless. In 1946, the Schachts were beside themselves and did not know which way to turn. There was no way that their school could run without a director and administrative leadership, not only during the regular school year but also during summer-school programming. The Schachts did not want to fail after coming so far, and they dreaded the thought of turning any child away or leaving any behind. But help was on the way, and a new chapter of the school would soon unfold.

Two

WHERE EVERYBODY IS SOMEBODY

Herb Schacht was the youngest of the family brood and was a soldier returning home after a three-year hitch in the US Army. He served as a medical-surgical technician and was honorably discharged in February 1946. Upon Herb's arrival, he agreed to help out temporarily at the school until his parents found a full-time director. Little did he know at the time that his leadership would become legendary for decades to come, and he would launch Waterford Country School into national prominence.

Herb graduated from high school at age 15 and earned a degree in animal husbandry from the University of Connecticut. Herb was remembered as a good student, a pupil who took pride in his work and was always punctual with his assignments. He learned to live with a serious and chronic asthma condition and never let it dampen his upbeat disposition. Herb was a friendly sort and popular among his peers. He told those around him that he sought adventure in his life and wanted to visit faraway places. Of his career interests, he was adamant about what he did not want to do. He had no intention of entering the field of education and vowed that he would never become a teacher or an administrator. In fact, he made it clear to several friends in his inner circle that deep down, he never really liked school.

This c. 1931 photograph captures Henry and Herb taking their trusty steads for a side-by-side horseback ride into the woods at Waterford Country School. The countryside purchased by the school offered several horse trails to follow, the favorite being one that curled past the cornfields and apple trees, then deep into the forest. They often rode side-by-side in the early morning, a time when deer, rabbits, squirrels, and other wildlife greeted them in the stillness of the forest trail. Henry and Herb found horseback riding as lively as it was energetic. The ride was made even more invigorating by the two of them commandeering their mounts outside the corral and away from the confines of the farm. They both reported seeing more, feeling more, and appreciating the splendor of the natural beauty surrounding them.

It came as no secret that Herb really did not want to be where or what his parents hoped he would be. He had fulfilled his military obligation to his country and looked forward to finding a little time for himself. He wanted a taste of freedom on his own terms and there were so many parts of the world he wanted to see. He had witnessed his parents' struggles and sacrifices and seriously doubted whether he could handle the challenges the school posed, particularly the demands of farm life.

A new director never came to Herb's rescue that first year. To his credit, Herb put his best foot forward managing the school and recalled how he learned something new every day. The youngsters helped in the barn milking cows, gathering eggs, and carrying wood for the furnace. Along the way, he taught them how to express their appreciation for things that were done for them or given to them, placing an emphasis on gratitude and politeness. In time, Herb had fun and liked what he was doing. He enjoyed the children, appreciated the staff he worked alongside, and loved the countryside.

Herb continued his stay on the farm, directing the newly named Waterford Country School, supervising the staff, and teaching the children. He was visible to all and became an able teacher, utilizing Ettie's educational philosophy of how happiness created the emergence of fulfillment. He encouraged the more able students to help less abled classmates, and he advocated to his staff the importance of praise and encouragement. He instilled the motto that "Everybody Is Somebody." The early years flew by but came to a standstill when he met Emily Capo, a summer camp nurse. The two married in 1951 (right), making their home on the main grounds, about 50 feet from the main building. Together Herb and Emily (below) raised seven children: Thomas, Eileen, Barbara, Debbie, DD, Pam, and Robert.

Ettie Schacht, pictured here sharing a dance with son Herb at her 87th birthday celebration, was a pioneer in promoting the education of challenged students. Ettie taught Herb the importance of making a complete commitment to each child, giving a sense of belonging and acceptance to those looking for help. She believed that the children would become the teachers, showing them what the teachers needed, but only if the teachers would take the time to look and listen. In times of crisis, helpers need to ride out the storm and listen carefully and identify the needs of the troubled youngster and find ways to establish trust. Although Ettie stayed in New York, she remained an advisor and provided the staff at Waterford Country School with endless amounts of guidance and advice.

Four generations of the Schacht family have serviced Waterford Country School. Ettie and Henry's son Herb (pictured here with his wife, Emily) became the permanent camp director. Emily was a camp nurse and, later, a volunteer school nurse. Ettie and Henry's daughter Rita and her husband, Bo Saunders, were co-directors of the Buckingham School in Brooklyn and Camp Waterford in the summer. Grandchildren continued the familial commitment to WCS. They became child-care workers, psychologists, counselors, swimming instructors, clinical directors, board of trustee members, and administrative assistants to the development director. Suffice it to say that the Schacht family history is legendary not only in the creation of Waterford Country School but also in its continuing acclamation as a treatment and education center.

Outdoor learning infuses a desire among children to explore, discover, and learn about our natural world. From its earliest beginnings, Waterford Country School stressed the importance of encouraging children to be curious and active learners. The pioneers of WCS stressed that early outdoor education fosters in youngsters a lifelong connection to the natural world. The lessons learned outdoors, from the joys of discovery to the motivation to discover and explore, enables youngsters to see the intrigue and purpose of true learning. Planting the seeds of curiosity, the plant and animal world motivates young learners to explore and experiment, in the process boosting concentration and academic engagement. Combined, this creates a platform for learning and opens the gateway for new skills and interests.

At the time, the school was building a training program for those students who were physically able to perform farm tasks. The able students were carefully placed in those work assignments in which they could experience success. In this photograph, an older student milks one of the cows. The milk that the farm group handled was the school's entire source of milk. The students experienced a great sense of achievement and responsibility for the role they played in the school's overall operation.

Creating bonds with a farm animal was encouraged and praised by the staff. The students were taught to always treat farm animals with care and respect. It was believed that developing positive feelings about farm animals impacted a student's self-esteem and self-confidence. More importantly, learning to care for an animal, such as treating it kindly and patiently, likely provides training in learning to treat people the same way.

All students working with farm animals received instruction on general farm safety, handling and caring for the animals, as well as safety at all times with the animals. When working jobs on the farm, students are assigned tasks they can undertake with success. A diverse assortment of chores is available. For example, the above photograph captures a student tending to fenced-in livestock while the image below captures a stray cow being coaxed back to the herd. Working with farm animals helps to develop responsible behavior in the students tending them as well as promoting an ethic of compassion and humaneness. Such teaching principles are still in practice today, with farm animals and wildlife being the catalyst for fostering hands-on learning opportunities.

The power of the human-animal bond became the cornerstone for the WCS farm program in the early years. Pot-bellied pigs have always been a favorite among students, largely because they give back numerous therapeutic benefits. They are affectionate companions and have always demonstrated an easy temperament. They are flea-free, friendly, and inexpensive to feed. They love the human touch and readily roll over for a tummy rub, as well as snuggle with visitors.

According to Ettie Schacht, an appreciation of all living things provides valuable lessons not only about animals but also about life in general, including such passages as reproduction, birth, illness, and death. Visiting the farm animals as often as possible created enjoyment as well as empathy, together creating a valuable learning lesson. Ettie often remarked that for children to learn, they need to be happy, and in order to be happy, they needed to trust. She believed positive exposure and relationships with farm animals, in turn, promote trusting relationships with those in one's surroundings.

Learning to farm was one of the major educational endeavors of the school. Those students deemed physically fit and psychologically able were chosen to participate in farming activities. Selection was based on one's work history, readiness to work with others in a group, and willingness to accept and carry out assigned chores. There were many tasks based on the seasonal phases of farming, such as seeding (left) and tilling the soil (below). The summer months required cultivating, harvesting, and other seasonal chores, such as those a commercial farm would be engaged in during the year.

The fruits of one's labor were always celebrated on the farm. Accomplishment and a reward of one's toils always struck a high note among the students, such as those pictured above. Working on the farm had a positive impact on the participants, the students demonstrating more responsible and courteous behaviors away from the farm. Participants also exhibited a satisfactory working knowledge of agricultural skills, keeping in mind each student's capability level. Combined, the agricultural experience provided convincing evidence that students needed programs such as these to help pave the way to adulthood. To achieve this, the need was for programs that could provide a sense of responsibility, knowledge of doing a worthwhile job, and a feeling of immediate achievement and self-worth. Herb Schacht's farming legacy is carried on today by Rob "Digga" Schacht and his wife, Teresa, and his son Sam. As an entrepreneur, Digga built a thriving business close to campus called Hunts Brook Farm that helps feed the local community and WCS with a bounty of healthy, delectable produce.

When warmer weather prevailed, Camp Waterford opened its doors to local summer school children and youth. From its earliest beginnings, a structured and balanced summer camp was offered, each day filled with a wide range of activities. Early on, the summer programs were directed by Rita Schacht and her husband, Bo Saunders. Each morning, a school bugle boy sounded reveille before dawn's break (above). Over the years, the school bugler was usually admired by fellow students for sheer musical talent, but when reveille blasted each morning at the crack of dawn, collective groans and grumbling could be heard, in some cases prompting cries of outright indignation. Of course, in due time a structured life became secondhand as the unfamiliar became familiar and children learned to adjust to each day's expectations and routines. In the photograph below, campers meet in the school's recreational hall to preview the day's activities.

Regular exercise was a staple of the day for the children and teens attending Waterford Country School. Exercise was not only good for one's physical health but also supported emotional and mental health. Usually, structured exercises were scheduled for the mornings and were led by qualified physical education instructors (above and at right). It was maintained that a morning workout was especially beneficial because it boosted energy levels to start the day. An exercise regimen was especially beneficial for children with a disability. The WCS staff was trained to support disabled youngsters in being as active as possible. The staff avoided comparing disabled children with other youngsters or shaming them if they were not able to do as much. Instead, the staff was taught to reinforce and celebrate their achievements and successes.

Campers fell in love with lake Cuheca. The lake was privately owned by the school and was the perfect secluded and peaceful setting for both children and staff. Motorized boats were not allowed on the lake, making it ideal for youngsters wanting to explore the lake via canoe or rowboat. The lake offered several piers, a diving platform, picnic tables, a raft, and a sandy beachfront. Campers discovered that they were surrounded by a lush, beautiful forest with clearly marked trails.

Bo Saunders (center), one of the summer camp directors, is flanked by the school's swimming instructors and lifeguards. All have been trained in rescue techniques, life-saving, and water safety. When on duty, lifeguards were always instructed to be out of the water and guarding during any use of the lakefront, including swimming, diving, canoeing, and boating.

"Kick kick kick kick kick." The sound of this sequence of instruction would ring out across the lake and through the woods. Of course, they were commands directed toward the youngest campers—the "tadpoles" and "guppies"—learning how to swim. Here, the youngsters are kicking together while holding on to the side of a pier. Instructors would repeatedly use the same "kick" word or would offer kick songs and melodies when they wanted kicking to commence.

Older children utilized the diving platform and were allowed to swim in deeper water under the watchful eye of a lifeguard. Swimming instructors were also on hand to ensure that each camper felt safe and secure. Swimmers were divided into subgroups consisting of children with similar swimming abilities, enabling instruction to progress at a uniform pace. Campers were also scheduled for "free" swim sessions every day.

Older youngsters were taught the basics for treating drowning victims, at least according to the teachings of the day. The ever-present Bo Saunders was assigned to oversee the teaching techniques (second from left) and added many tips from his extensive military background. Readers should recognize, though, that this is not today's prescribed protocol for treating drowned swimmers. In this photograph, certified lifeguards and instructors give instructions to the older children paired up, with one rescuer and one victim. The victim is in a prone position, and the rescuer uses external upper back compressions to hopefully create an open airway.

Boating was another favorite lake activity. Thanks to the efforts of Herb Schacht, a flotilla of rowboats and canoes were always available at the shoreside. Always accompanied by an adult, the rowboats enjoyed calm waters and scenic displays of the surrounding woodlands. In this particular photograph, the counselor demonstrates clear command of the craft while the child in the stern shows no appetite for rowing while the one in the bow is much too busy napping to offer any kind of assistance.

Rowing on the lake often brought challenges to the young campers. Here, instructions from a counselor are delivered to young boaters. The boats were often used to race from the raft to the shoreline. A counselor would supervise in each boat.

Being able to launch a canoe may seem like an easy feat, but campers at WCS needed to first learn safety measures. First and foremost, no canoe or boat could leave the shore without an experienced camping instructor on board. Being accompanied by a camp counselor with experience made learning easier, faster, and safer. Preparation was also key to any outdoor activity with youngsters. Of course, wearing a life jacket was vital. Counselors agreed that anyone can start canoeing without much training. The training focused on getting in a canoe safely from the beach, without tipping. Teaching tips focused on using paddling techniques that enhanced stability, paddling in sync with one's partner, and keeping one's paddle shaft vertical.

Away from the water, softball was a popular sport for the players as well as the spectators (see the bleachers behind the backstop filled with interested onlookers). While the games were played for fun and enjoyment, they also presented camp counselors with an opportunity to help youngsters improve their skills in hitting, fielding, and base running. At the forefront of the teaching moment, though, was building a camper's confidence and teaching good sportsmanship.

Softball games between counselors and campers were popular at Camp Waterford. When the weather was nice, games got underway, and it was enjoyable watching the campers play the game while simultaneously improving their baseball skills. Spectators always enjoyed watching a camper get the game-winning hit or making a game-saving play. The end result of such a competition was that campers were taught the importance of teamwork, enthusiasm, and motivation.

Sporting competition or intramural activity was at the heart of many campers during summers gone by. Older campers (above) and younger campers (below) enjoyed this friendly competition. WCS encouraged healthy competition among participants, the instructors encouraging the value of teamwork, camaraderie, and goodwill among the campers. In other words, the supervisors believed that sports built strong bonds within the camp, which in turn fostered a sense of belonging and togetherness. Meanwhile, the athletic skills, be it the mastery of football or soccer, allowed campers to develop psychomotor skills and fine-tune motor skills involving coordination, movement, strength, dexterity, and speed. As far as intramural participants were concerned, sports were a casual way to join organized athletics. The staff maintained that all youth had a need to belong, become a team member, and build relationships.

In addition to engaging in physically challenging activities, developmentally abled children were introduced to less strenuous forms of exercise, such as dancing or other movement exercises. At the time, dancing was thought to improve youngsters' muscle tone, strength, endurance, and fitness. Among young children especially, dancing and movement exercises proved to help with balance and coordination. WCS teachers maintained that it was important for youngsters to engage in opportunities requiring them to move. Exercise, like food, is a fundamental part of a child's physical growth. Exercise enables youngsters to build stronger muscles and bones. Beyond enhancing a child's mental health and mood, exercise also elevates a child's self-esteem.

Tucked away in the hills of Quaker Hill, the days of autumn became shorter and the weather a bit colder. The trees cascading the surrounding area created fiery leaf colors, providing a splendid background to the school's campus and marking upcoming preparations for Halloween, a favorite celebration among WCS students. Many students believed nightmarish ghouls lurked in the closet or under their bed, and others shuddered at the sight of nighttime shadows on the wall or cobwebs dangling from their ceilings. But Waterford Country School happily celebrated Halloween as a time for dressing up in costumes, participating in various contests and activities, and consuming sweets. Here, WCS students and staff congregate and show off their costumes, from police officers and princesses to cowboys and skeletons.

"So, tell me, how long have you two fellas been camping?" One can only imagine the conversation going on with these boys. Beyond the swimming, hiking, baseball, and other camp activities, campers had free blocks of time and the chance to get to know one another. Summer camp was a place where friendships were made, where youngsters had the freedom to be themselves away from the pressures of school or constraints at home.

Most of the time, the summer camp kept youngsters on the move. But sometimes, many wished to find a bit of reclusiveness, such as what these three girls discovered sitting on rocks next to a nearby brook. Whether it be casting a fishing line into the water or just engaging in quiet conversation, spots like this recognized the value of a little peace and quiet amidst busy camp life. As such, this hideaway enabled youngsters to not only enjoy each other's company but also feel more connected to nature.

Camp life took huge amounts of patience from the camp teachers. Something as simple as preparing snacks and encouraging youngsters to take turns and being respectful to others required constant monitoring. Mixed-age groupings often meant that youngsters were frequently rambunctious, with short attention spans and little self-control. The notion that every child is different made the toils of teaching even more challenging. Competent staff members were able to clearly state expectations and behaviors that the children could understand. WCS supervisors agreed that a patient nature, combined with a sense of humor, helped teachers handle the ups and downs of camp life, creating, in turn, a setting of acceptance and happiness among the children.

Today and yesteryear, a nursing station was an integral part of the school's operation and its student services. The school nurse attended to sick or injured campers as well as administered medications to all campers and staff. In addition to the camp nurse, an on-call camp doctor lived a short distance away and a hospital, if needed, was located in New London. The camp nurse also collaborated with staff on a regular basis to provide a healthy camp environment. In a camp setting, a wide range of accidents and illnesses can occur, including insect bites, allergic reactions, abrasions, lacerations, fractures, and other types of injuries. Other complaints were sore throats, homesickness, splinters, sprains, and upper respiratory tract infections. Camp nurses were trained to deal with all.

A wide range of sports activities was made available to youngsters every day, meeting a wide range of individual preferences. The schedule was designed for the campers to learn and develop their skills in the sports they liked in a positive, supportive atmosphere. It was understood by the counselors that youngsters engaged in sports because they wanted to have fun and get to know their new friends better. The adults took genuine pride in fostering a buoyant spirit every day and recognized that sports were an outlet for the campers. Sports gave them opportunities to exercise and learn not only how to succeed but also how to handle defeat.

Archery at WCS was a popular sport for youngsters and teens of all ages. It was also an activity promoted by camp counselors because of the many benefits it offered to participants. At a simple level, the teaching of archery encouraged listening as well as engaging with instructions and safety rules. The sport enabled participants to build on their developing skills and enjoy the satisfaction that comes from it, which in turn builds confidence in their skills. Having confidence at a young age through archery can help promote positive mental health. As far as skills were concerned, archery required concentration and eye-hand coordination. It can help build different muscles of the body such as the chest, back, and shoulder muscles. When a person draws a bow, it strengthens the body's core muscles and improves balance and stability. All of these benefits were invaluable when one considered youngsters were well on their way to developing their physical attributes.

Under Herb Schacht's tenure as director, a concerted effort was made to build bridges to the surrounding community. Local residents were encouraged to visit Waterford Country School and tour the school grounds. The staff and students at the school also volunteered as helpers in area surroundings. The school offered free land use to Boy Scouts, Girl Scouts, public schools, churches, and other nonprofit organizations. The public was also invited to school events such as the Circus and Fair Day (left), an event marked by various amusements, contests, refreshments, and games of skills (below). The Circus and Fair Day proved to be a predecessor to today's enormously popular Family Fun Days at the school.

At the Circus and Fair Day, participants, as well as spectators, enjoyed the races put on display. Above, youngsters line up and put two feet in a potato sack to hop their way to a finish line. Contestants must keep both feet in the sack and at least one hand on the sack at all times. The sack must be held as close to the waist as possible and was not allowed to fall below the knees. Joining in on the fun was WCS staff and residents on the front lawn of the campus, showing off their dancing and musical skills (below).

Apart from summer camp sessions, Waterford Country School students remained the focus of attention and the recipients of programming and instruction aimed at personal and emotional growth. Each student learned to gain control of his or her life and experienced the joys of achievement and success. In these photographs taken in an arts and crafts class, youngsters are engaged in painting pottery and birdhouses. Involvement in activities such as these promotes skills and creates happier, healthier, and more productive lives. Waterford Country School believed such positive traits should be the birthright of every youngster and the heritage for future generations.

Whether it be indoor or outdoor learning activities, the school lauds its teachers and their dedication to student engagement and success. Their instruction is driven by respect for others, compassion, and hope among students of all levels. Whether it be the teaching of sawing wood and stacking it or gathering crops, teachers possess the skills and talents to spark positive change in students and enhance their overall confidence and well-being. At the foundation of their pedagogy, teachers possess a determined and distinguishable work ethic that embraces students' social, emotional, behavioral, and learning differences.

Both young and old students were given chores around the grounds based on ability and interest. The assigned work was a learning-by-doing experience. Youngsters fine-tuned their gardening, painting, and carpentry skills while in close proximity to a staff member, who will provide assistance if needed and serve as a role model. The above photograph displays a lawn being landscaped by a group of boys while below a young student is seen applying stain to an outside bench. One of the enduring hallmarks of the school is that work assignments are where the camaraderie between students often blossoms into a group of friends sharing an experience. In short, learning by doing is a vehicle for bringing students together.

Summer campers were expected to maintain cleanliness and exhibit good personal hygiene habits during their stay at Waterford Country School. More specifically, showering, practicing dental hygiene, wearing clean clothing, maintaining clean bedding, and keeping clothing in provided lockers were a must. The nails and hair of each camper required attention as well as the skin. The floor was to be swept on a regular basis, and the bunkhouse was to be kept tidy at all times. Inspections were conducted on a regular basis. Demerits and awards were given by camp supervisors. Close inspection of the above image reveals that this group of boys received a top inspection award in 1949, the plaque proudly displayed on the bunk's entryway.

"*En garde! Prêts?*" The French command for "On guard! Ready?" could be heard for many years among WCS campers participating in fencing. Fencing classes were quickly filled to capacity and consisted of instruction (above) as well as individual training and competition (below). Fencing is an enjoyable sport for campers and promotes quick thinking, balance, speed, and agility. Instructors emphasize mental and physical strategies that build confidence as well as self-discipline and good sportsmanship. Fencing on a regular basis promotes bone and muscle mass, not to mention overall fitness and wellness. At Waterford Country School, every fencing bout starts with a salute to one's opponent and ends with a handshake.

Do too many cooks spoil the broth? Not at Waterford Country School, where children and teenagers were encouraged and even recruited to participate in the preparation of food and beverages. The staff strongly believed that working alongside qualified food personnel was a way to build self-esteem, teach them the importance of following directions, and introduce youngsters to a variety of fresh foods and interesting ways of preparing and cooking those ingredients. Young students were introduced to a variety of simple tasks, like mixing, counting eggs, stirring, washing, slicing, or simple chopping. Older students were taught to, among other tasks, peel raw potatoes, ginger, mangoes, and other washed fruits and vegetables. Executive director Herb Schacht (below) was known to show up—often without advance warning—to help on the serving line as well as to help the students prepare the food.

Congregate dining at the school was a means to practice social etiquette and a vehicle to foster healthy interpersonal relationships. This photograph captures the dining hall as it existed around 1952. Among other goals, both indoor and outdoor dining-hall settings encouraged respect and compassion for the differences that existed between students and staff and engendered a sense of community. The dining hall was envisioned as a routine, a consistent environment that made children and teenagers feel secure and safe. Especially important was that congregate dining enabled students to utilize the skills and competencies they had learned in therapy and apply them to everyday interactions, such as sitting down with others and enjoying a meal.

In the image above, a professional dance performance takes place on the outside green. Dance practices and recitals were popular activities at WCS. Through dance, it was maintained that youngsters developed a greater range of movement while developing the ability to work within different spaces. Student dance recitals showcased at the school were popular events, as seen below. Dancers learned to interpret the effect their movement has on the world around them. Dancing also improved coordination, especially at a time when the body was rapidly developing in an ever-changing and evolving environment. Instructors note that movement combinations increase memory, order, and sequencing skills. Involvement in dancing also increases self-esteem, a vital component of learning and achievement. Finally, dance allows children to reinvent themselves and be whom they want to be in a positive, supportive environment.

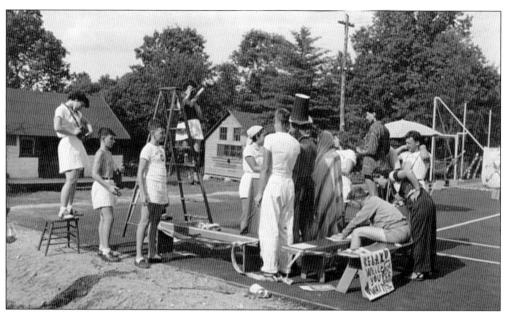

The above photograph captures a student theater troupe preparing for a performance to be held later in the evening. The actual performance later on consisted of many actors and stagehands and attracted considerable audience attention (below). WCS teachers and staff administrators felt that live performances enabled children to appreciate people of all kinds and how to respect other points of view. Looking back at historic performances, each production brought a story with a unique viewpoint, ranging from stories about ballerinas, siblings, new students, elves, cultures, and characters from all over the world. Those overseeing the productions felt it was important for students to learn about different kinds of people and aspects of life, in the process offering a glimpse of other people's lives. In this way, theater enabled students to step into someone else's shoes and see life from a different point of view.

What do you get when you combine a Briggs and Stratton motor, an asphalt surface, and nine students holding hands while balancing themselves on roller skates? Why, teenagers from the 1950s rockin' the night away. It looks as though these students are getting warmed up to play "Crack the whip," a game where the leader establishes the direction and the rest of the skaters follow like a whip. Inevitably, one or two skaters lose their grip, and the whip breaks. Those skaters are out of the game as the whip reconnects and the game continues. Sometimes, this game gets a tad rowdy and overzealous, especially when a camp counselor is distracted or not paying attention.

In 1968, the Buckingham School in New York was sold, and the Schacht family, recognizing that the Connecticut school needed to take on a different structure in order to continue serving future generations of children, created a nonprofit corporation with a community board of Trustees in 1969 and transferred for a token amount the present campus, buildings, equipment, and programs to the new organization, Waterford Country School, Inc. Instead of family proprietorship, the school was now governed and run by a board of trustees, increasingly drawn from the community. Present at the formal signing of the incorporation documents (above, from left to right) were attorney Robert P. Anderson Jr., Emily C. Schacht, Rita S. Saunders, and Ettie T. Schacht. Below, Herb Schacht signs the necessary documents.

Three

CHANGING OF THE GUARD

In 1981, Herb Schacht (right) retired as executive director of the school and was replaced by David B. Moorehead (left) from New Jersey. Herb continued to advocate for children long after he retired. Moorehead had previously served as executive director of the Baptist Children's Services in Philadelphia, Pennsylvania. He holds a bachelor's degree in speech/history from Millikin University in Decatur, Illinois; a master's degree in speech pathology/special education from Trenton State University, Trenton New Jersey; and a master's degree in social work from Rutgers University in New Brunswick, New Jersey.

Dave Moorehead was a visionary and set his sights on upgrading, renovating, and expanding Waterford Country School. Working closely with the board of trustees and his leadership team, he carefully assessed what had gone well in the school's storied past, what the school needed to keep and improve to best serve the students, and what the school no longer needed. In the image above, Moorehead (center) shares ideas with Gary Saunders (left), a member of the board of trustees as well as the development committee, and state senator Andrea Stillman (right), a member of the school's board of directors. William Martin (below) served as assistant executive director during Moorehead's 31-year tenure. The tandem worked to bring many positive changes to the school. Martin was appointed executive director in 2012.

Moorehead was a visible presence both on and off campus. One of his motivations upon arrival was to increase the school's involvement in the surrounding communities so that it would be seen as a multifaceted resource to everyone. From the beginning he wanted to create connections with community members, paying particular attention to partnership possibilities. Here, Moorehead (left) is seen talking with Gloria Hatfield (middle), the school's development secretary, and Carl Bridges (right), a former board of trustees member.

It is not often that one can strike up a casual chat with a National Football League legend. Moorehead does just that as he watches a horse show held on campus with Otto Graham, a Hall of Famer with the Cleveland Browns. Otto believed in the mission of WCS and along with his wife, Beverly, helped with many building and developmental projects at the school, particularly the Otto Graham Gymnasium and Activity Center. Beverly was the first president of the WCS Foundation, a group organized to help raise funds for campus renovation. We'll revisit the gymnasium project a bit later in the book.

The previous photograph captured Dave Moorehead and Otto Graham conversing at the Connie Lord Riding Ring. The ring was constructed in memory of its namesake, who passed away in 2018. Lord, a member of the school's development committee, also launched the WCS Horse Show, which was held for several decades. The ring is now used for a school-sponsored equine education and therapeutic horseback-riding program.

In its heyday, the WCS Horse Show attracted hundreds of spectators and riders throughout New England, and its operation involved staff members and volunteers from the region. Riders competed in such classes as saddle seat, hunt seat, junior English, beginner's walk-trot, pony, western, junior western, stock, and gymkhana. Trophies and ribbons were awarded to winners in each class. All proceeds benefitted the school.

In 1982, attorney Robert P. Anderson Jr., chairman of WCS's board of trustees, announced a $3.5 million development program for the school. A three-year, fund-raising drive was called the Waterford Country School Foundation, headed by Kenneth E. Grube and Otto E. Graham. The master plan for the development program, named, "Toward a Century of Service," combined the use of terrain, natural resources, and renovated existing structures with cottage-style living units, a residential treatment center, a classroom building, and a gymnasium and fitness center. At the bedrock of the development project was a carefully cultivated plan to construct life-learning experiences and services that best meet the needs of multihandicapped children and youth.

The construction of four cottage-style living units was part of the initial phase of the development project (above). A dedication of the four cottages (the below photograph shows one such residence) took place in November 1989. The cottages were situated around a cul-de-sac to simulate a residential neighborhood and were designed to create a sense of security and stability for the students. Also, it was anticipated the new residences would promote a feeling of family-style activities deemed important for the well-being of the residents. A dedication plaque mounted in each of the cottage's foyers displayed the names of persons prominent in WCS's history: the Schacht family, pioneers of the school; Beatrice Holt Rosenthal, a board of trustee member; Frank Schlossberg, father and grandfather of building and hardware supply owners offering assistance in WCS's development project; and Seymour and Patricia Adelman, who contributed the funds for the construction of the cottages.

Each cottage was designed to create a clean, healthy, homelike, functional environment for the students to live in, learn about themselves, get along with others, and understand and follow rules and expectations. In short, planners wanted to create a setting where students could work together on valuable life skills. Each cottage-type living unit has two single bedrooms and six double bedrooms. Shared spaces include the living room and game room. Both rooms were designed large enough to accommodate all the residents at the same time. In so doing, staff and students could make the most of their time together, building relationships and personal skills as they cook breakfast and dinner together, take care of their spaces, and enjoy leisure time.

A groundbreaking ceremony for the Thomas P. Bent Emergency Shelter was held in June 1991. The shelter was part of the school's development plan and was designed to serve as a home and counseling facility for children or youth from southeastern Connecticut who require immediate placement. Participating in the ceremonies included Dave Moorehead, WCS executive director (second from left); Mark Wolman, project manager (second from right); and Bill Martin, WCS assistant executive director (far right).

Construction of the Bent Shelter, another part of the campus expansion plan, was completed in January 1993. The shelter was made possible through a grant from the Pequot Community Foundation in memory of the late Thomas P. Bent. Mr. Bent's wishes were to offer assistance and serve troubled children and youth in the surrounding area. The 6,000-foot building offered living quarters for up to fourteen clients. While in placement, a support network would be developed with other community agencies. The goal of the shelter was to return clients to their own homes or other appropriate placement ideally in a few days but with a goal of 30 to 60 days.

In years gone by, WCS students and teachers were often huddled together in cramped quarters, making student learning and teacher effectiveness a struggle (above). Recognizing the need for an improved academic climate, an integral part of the school's development project was creating a new and enriched learning environment. The culmination of these efforts was the introduction of the 1999 Levine Education Center (below). The school consists of two floors, eleven classrooms, a computer lab, and administrative offices. WCS students are children in kindergarten through 12th grade with specialized emotional and behavioral needs. Responding to such needs, teachers and staff strive for close relationships with students and involve families as much as possible. The foundation of this pedagogy is that each moment in the classroom as well as other educational experiences, such as those available at the outdoor experiential center, can utilize teaching moments as opportunities for students' personal growth and academic success.

Modern classroom settings in the Levine Education Center enable each classroom to be set up based on what is necessary to meet learning objectives. The school maintains a low student-to-teacher ratio, allowing highly personalized instruction. Beyond the teachers, the school has access to a qualified support staff including, among others, a school psychologist, a reading therapist, a speech therapist, an occupational therapist, a reading specialist, clinicians/social workers, and one-on-one mentors. In addition to academic instruction, the education program provides creative ideas for personal achievement and improvement initiatives. The ultimate goal is to enable students to better meet the challenges they face in their school, family, and community.

A surprise 85th-birthday party took place for a legend at Waterford Country School. With lips sealed, loved ones whisked Herb Schacht from his home and delivered him to the school where a congregation of teachers, staff, and students awaited. When he emerged from the car, cheers and applause erupted from the crowd. Banners and streamers were everywhere. Everyone wore specially designed tee-shirts with Herb's photograph displayed on the front accompanied by the caption, "Herb is my hero. Herb hired me." Cardboard enlargements of Herb's smiling face were also affixed to wooden shafts and waved back and forth by both young and old well-wishers. Speakers at the celebration included, among others, executive director David Moorehead and Robert Anderson, chairman of the board of trustees. Following refreshments, the group joined hands in traditional WCS fashion and created the Friendship Circle. It was a day everyone would remember. This photograph features Herb being flanked by (left to right) Sharon Butcher, director of education; Bill Martin, assistant executive director; and Anne Adams, physical education teacher.

One of the highlights of WCS's education program is the daily inclusion of outdoor experiential education into the lives of students. Students are actively involved in the outdoor program and create special bonds with the animals that are gateways for building relationships with staff and fellow students. Students have the opportunity to learn how to care for a variety of domestic animals and exotic pets who come to Waterford Country School for rehabilitation or retirement. Each student spends at least one period a day to enhance the overall educational experience at Waterford Country School.

Due to the unending support of Dave Moorehead and Bill Martin for outdoor experiential education, the program mushroomed and became a shining jewel in the crown of Waterford Country School. All of this was orchestrated by Rick McPherson, a pioneer in the founding of the center. Rick joined the WCS's ranks in 1976 and rose through the ranks to become the director of the experiential education center. In this image, McPherson is seen conducting an outdoor learning "show-and-tell" lesson for WCS students. The rapt attention of the audience says it all.

The construction of the challenge ropes climbing tower and course was dedicated to the memory of Ken Grube, a board of trustees member, humanitarian, and visionary in the development of services for children and families. The course has eight high elements and fifteen low team-building elements on Lake Cuheca to increase participants' self-esteem and promote a sense of unity, trust, and mutual support in group activities. The course caters to WCS programs, local schools and organizations, sports teams, and company retreats. The construction of the ropes tower (right) was designed to offer students low rope and high rope challenges. The ropes course offers a challenging opportunity for the body and mind. With trained facilitators present, students are encouraged to put their skills to the test and work together to learn more about themselves and their peers (below). As far as safety measures are concerned, first-aid and emergency response equipment are always accessible to staff, appropriate staff/participant ratios are always maintained, and facilitators are positioned to maximize participant supervision at all times.

Rose Lodge, a beautiful log cabin located near lake Cuheca, was dedicated in loving memory of Rose Pasnik Slosberg and Harold J. Slosberg in 1999. Rose Lodge has been at the heart of the outdoor education center programs and has provided a rustic and peaceful ambiance for ropes programs, Camp Cuheca, company retreats, meetings, classes, training sessions, and special events throughout the community.

In 2010, the outdoor education center was dedicated to Rick McPherson, who retired in 2015 and left behind a legacy of inspiration, learning, and fun. His contributions were many, including an animal sanctuary, ropes course, a nature center, greenhouses, and a federally licensed wildlife rehabilitation center. He was a visionary and taught those around him to be more observant of animals and our natural world. He will always be remembered as a person who loved animals, protected them from danger, and kept them healthy and content.

Four

WHATEVER IT TAKES

Bill Martin was hardly an unknown presence when he stepped up and became executive director of Waterford Country School in 2012. Over the years, he had distinguished himself at different levels as he climbed the agencies' hierarchal ladder. He had gone from a social service coordinator, director of child care, and assistant executive director before he was appointed to the school's top position. He holds a bachelor's degree from Fairleigh Dickinson University in New Jersey and a master's degree in human service administration from Antioch University in New Hampshire.

Martin was a devoted and charismatic leader who got everyone involved and excited about a vision for the school and the means to achieve it. The students adored him, the staff admired him, and the board of trustees believed in him. He was a familiar face on the campus and had that special knack for making every child and staff feel important and valued (above). At fundraisers and school social functions, his enthusiasm was as inspirational as it was unremitting (left). His staff always appreciated and applauded his transparency and praised the way he accentuated the positives and minimized the negatives. His sense of humor was contagious, and he truly believed that when you make workers happy, they become more productive. However, none of this implies that he was not a driven, goal-oriented leader. He embraced the mantra of "Whatever It Takes," a catchphrase coined by WCS's Sharon Butcher. During his tenure, he vowed to leave no stone unturned in making a difference in the lives of troubled children.

As executive director, Martin inspired his leadership team to always be involved with the legendary campus events, such as the friendship circle. The WCS leadership team Martin led could help him build on the past and navigate into the future. This treasured inner circle consisted of trusted and tested veterans, individuals skilled at their craft and more than ready to help the school move forward. Martin viewed this team as the critical moving parts enabling WCS to reap success with the projects at hand but also as a team keeping a watchful eye on future projects and developments waiting around the next corner.

The board of trustees establishes the "vision" for Waterford Country School and as such is responsible for reviewing pending changes and making adjustments that are in the best interests of the school. Put another way, the board is an appointed group of individuals saddled with the overall responsibility for the management of Waterford Country School. This responsibility encompasses carefully contemplated decisions made on the school's behalf. In this photograph, the school's board of trustees poses with Bill Martin and Martha Holden (both, left), a guest from Cornell University.

The Mercado Recreation Hall (above), known as the "gym," was an all-purpose building used for many different events. As a makeshift basketball court, it left much to be desired. The roof leaked, the building had poor ventilation, the court was undersized (left), and dead spots in the flooring made dribbling nearly impossible. The basket rims were unsteady, and the gym smelled of dirty socks, sweat, and other mephitic odors. The ceiling was also too low. One particular game was attended by the board of trustees chairman Robert P. Anderson. He recalled in that game how a player launched a long shot, surely a three-pointer if it went in. On its way up, though, the ball hit the ceiling and dropped harmlessly to the floor below. Anderson recalled thinking how frustrating that must have been for the player, a frustration the boy surely did not need.

Before Dave Moorehead retired, he had successfully guided fundraising with Martin to the tune of $1,779,771 for the construction of the Otto Graham Gymnasium and Activity Center. This amounted to about 85 percent of the total cost when Bill Martin arrived, and he immediately continued fundraising efforts to secure the remaining $503,229. When that goal was achieved, a groundbreaking ceremony took place on September 23, 2013. Martin emceed the program while twirling a basketball with deft ball-handling skill as he spoke (above).

In attendance at the ground breaking were members of the Graham family, WCS Board of Trustees, staff, volunteers, donors, and elected officials. Beverly Graham, Otto's wife, was given the proverbial gold shovel. To signify the start of construction, she raised the shovel, and an excavator took the first scoop. Guest speakers at the ceremony included Ryan Graham (Otto's grandson, standing behind Beverly, right), state senator Andrea Stillman, and state representative Betsy Ritter.

The ceremony marked the beginning of the construction process, beginning with the demolishment of the old recreation hall (above). Once the debris of the hall was removed, preliminary site grading was done to adjust the slope and elevation of the soil around the foundation. Given the unpredictable New England weather, fingers were crossed that winter storms would not interfere with the pouring and setting of the foundation. Luckily, there were no extended delays. Next, a skeleton frame of vertical steel columns and horizontal I-beams was constructed (below). The 15,900-square-foot project was undertaken by Kronenberger & Sons Restoration, Inc. The construction site sat on the main campus and was clearly visible from Hunts Brook Road, allowing both students and staff to watch daily progress. Bill Martin also offered the WCS staff and students the rare opportunity to climb on ladders with spotters below to sign personal messages on the rafters with large indelible markers before the interior insulation was sealed up for the future.

On October 22, 2014, staff, friends, and supporters attended the opening and dedication of the Otto Graham Gymnasium and Fitness Center. It was a heartfelt program where former executive director David Moorehead, Sen. Andrea Stillman, Rep. Betsy Ritter, and Otto's grandson Ryan all shared their stories. Bill Martin, the executive director, then announced a launch ceremony in which members of the Graham family, donors, politicians, the founding family, town officials, and the designers/builders all took shots at the basket. The new gymnasium (above) includes three basketball courts with professional glass backboards and breakaway rims, the WCS logo at center court, a fitness center (named after the late board of trustees member Gary Saunders), locker rooms, offices, storage, a stage, a conference training center, a classroom, and a lobby where a large display of donors' names is placed next to Otto Graham's memorabilia and a captivating mural. Annual fundraising basketball games offering thunderous dunks and arching and floating three-pointers by impressive athletes include the Valentine Classic and WCS staff vs. local police departments. The new gymnasium, barn-like in appearance and painted rustic red with white trim (below), complements the existing buildings and grounds and was designed to enhance the picturesque WCS campus.

In April 2013, Bill Martin shepherded the acquisition of Connecticut Adoption Services just as Dave Moorehead had done in 1983 with WCS's foster-care services and other programming mergers. The adoption program is operated in the school's Norwich office, sharing space with the foster-care program. The adoption program complements WCS's mission and fits nicely with its foster-care program, the principles of the training for both programs being quite similar. The transition was extremely successful as all of the programs and services of the former Connecticut Adoption & Family Services were able to continue without disruption. The acquisition of the adoption services joins other programs in WCS's outreach showcase: residential treatment, therapeutic boarding school, emergency shelter, Quality Parenting Center (QPC), special education (Kindergarten through 12th grade), Camp Cuheca Summer Camp, therapeutic foster care, outpatient mental health clinic, outdoor education, and wildlife rehabilitation. Pictured here is Addie, a husky-shepherd dog that is among 15 companion/therapy dogs on the WCS campus.

In 2009, Waterford Country School adopted Cornell University's CARE model. The model holds, at its core value, interpersonal relationships based upon respect, compassion, and hope among all persons at all levels. WCS focused on developing a team of staff who possessed the skills and talents enabling them to establish caring relationships with children and families leading towards positive change and the enhancement of their overall well-being. Based on six guiding principles, the CARE model is designed to influence the way residential childcare professionals think about working with children. The principles include being developmentally focused, family-involved, relationship-based, competence-centered, trauma-informed, and ecologically oriented. A reception hosted by Martha Holden and Bill Martin captures the pride of the formal connection. In the photograph above, Cornell's Martha Holden holds a special achievement award to Bill Martin, while the image to the right captures a celebration honoring WCS's connection to Cornell University.

A celebration marked the formal acknowledgment of Waterford Country School's partnership with Cornell University. Many of Waterford Country School's finest were on hand to join in on the celebration, including (left to right) Julianna Velazquez, development director; Emily Thomson, chief operations officer; Elena French, assistant director of development; and Lisa Duzy, director of foster care and community services. Overall, the crowd in attendance gushed with praise at Martin's role in achieving the Cornell-WCS connection, sharing their admiration and appreciation for his stewardship and dedication to the task at hand. Well-wishers had the opportunity to personally meet Martha Holden and learn of her international travels as well as her academic life at Cornell University. Many members of the leadership and supervisory teams became highly trained Cornell University CARE and TCI (Therapeutic Crisis Intervention) trainers. Sharon Butcher, tenured WCS principal, and Bill Martin have taught internationally as trainers and consultants for Cornell University, promoting the CARE and TCI models for other agencies to learn.

In November 2020, Cornell University presented the Eckenrode Award for Partner in Translational Research to Bill Martin of Waterford Country School. The Eckenrode Award is dedicated to honoring individuals who have played a vital partnership role with Cornell researchers to expand, strengthen, and speed connections between research, policy, and practice in the service of human development and wellbeing. Martin was recognized for his leadership role at Waterford Country School as well as creating a partnership with Cornell University's Residential Child Care Project. His efforts enabled WCS to become a critical partner in building the evidence base necessary for identifying areas for research and development of the CARE model on the use of high-risk interventions and psychometric medication on children in their care. The CARE model has been implemented in more than fifty organizations in five countries and is making a difference in the lives of children and families as well as the staff and agencies that work with them.

Waterford Country School's Nature Center and Children's Farm at the McPherson Outdoor Education Center have remained as popular as ever through the years. The center is home to about 100 domestic farm and small exotic animals. WCS's kindergarten–12th grade school and residential programs care for these animals as part of their daily routines and responsibilities. As new animals arrive at the center, the staff often ask the youngsters give a name to each animal. In this fashion, each animal and child have a story, each contact made providing an exercise in experiential learning. On a similar and intentionally yoked experience, WCS also offers Children's Farm activities, a program enabling students to further their contacts with the animals as well as visits to the campus greenhouse and its planting fields. Here, students may plan the garden, prepare the soil, select and plant the seeds, and reap the produce. Beyond its service to WCS students, both programs are often used as a therapeutic activity for residents of retirement or assisted living communities and local schools as a means to recreate the precious human-animal bond.

The Nature Center was dedicated by Ted Olynciew in honor of his brother, Thomas Olynciw, a WCS supporter and donor. Ted currently serves as the school's first vice chairman of the board of trustees, chairmen of the property committee, and project manager and builder for all WCS residential construction projects, farm buildings, and education/administration structures. He has served on the board of trustees for the last 37 years. His wife, Eileen Potkay Olynciw, is also a member of the school's board of trustees and development committee, as well as being a distinguished author and owner/agent of the Landmark Real Estate Agency. The two have championed the mission of WCS and will always be remembered for their tireless loyalty and devotion to the school.

In 2005, the WCS Children's Farm was dedicated in the name of James Morgan Miner (pictured far left). A nationally recognized school administrator in the Waterford public school sector, Miner began serving on the WCS Board of Trustees in 1975 and made numerous and valuable contributions over the years. He served actively on the nominating committee, property committee, personnel committee, and children's service committee. He will long be remembered for his many contributions to the school, not because he was obliged to do so, but because of his love for the school and the assistance it provides to troubled youngsters.

One of the most innovative and valuable components of Waterford Country School is its Wildlife Rehabilitation Program. Working in concert with the school's Nature Center and Children's Farm, the goal of the program is to provide care to sick, injured, and orphaned wild animals so that eventually they can be returned to their natural habitat. The Wildlife Rehabilitation Program serves as a key component of the mission of Waterford Country School. The program provides a model for children in treatment as they observe animals coming to a nurturing environment and being released into the wild. In this photograph, the director of outdoor education Ben Turner releases a barred owl rehabilitated by staff, students, and local volunteers. The WCS program is a federal and state-licensed program that provides students with the precious opportunity to learn about wildlife, nature, environmental issues, and human values.

The Wildlife Rehabilitation and Nature Resources Program offers a refuge where care is provided for sick or injured wild animals. Almost 200 injured animals per year are admitted into the Wildlife Rehabilitation Program. Many animals are treated and released while others become permanent residents on our campus if they need to remain in a sheltered environment. WCS also offers a mobile farm, an inside program featuring an educational presentation, and hands-on interaction with 8–12 small animals. The program can be used as a therapeutic activity for residents of retirement or assisted living communities to reconnect with the human-animal bond. The above photograph captures a student learning about a rescued hawk named Lincoln, while below, students observe rehabilitated birds of prey at the newly renovated wildlife rehabilitation center that was funded by the Community Foundation of Eastern Connecticut.

In 2012, Camp Cuheca returned to WCS after being surprisingly closed since 1969. The innovative, multifaceted summer day camp rose to its billing and promotion, specializing in adventure and animal-assisted therapy and activities for children and youth that needed individualized support. The camp was designed for those youngsters that might not

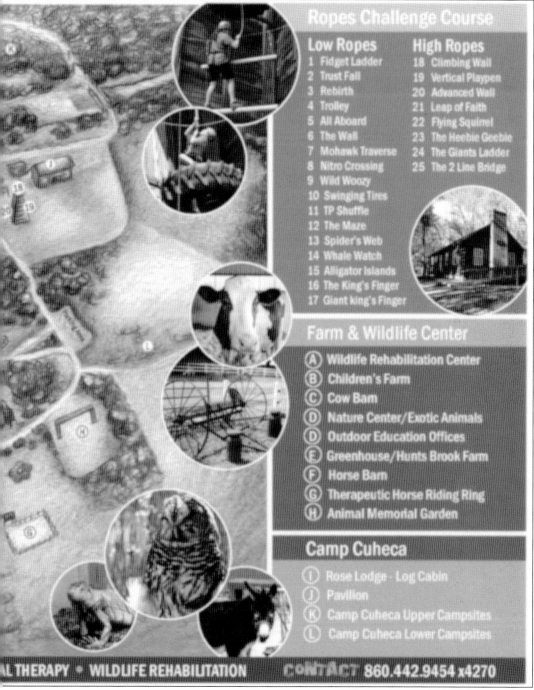

Ropes Challenge Course

Low Ropes	High Ropes
1 Fidget Ladder	18 Climbing Wall
2 Trust Fall	19 Vertical Playpen
3 Rebirth	20 Advanced Wall
4 Trolley	21 Leap of Faith
5 All Aboard	22 Flying Squirrel
6 The Wall	23 The Heebie Geebie
7 Mohawk Traverse	24 The Giants Ladder
8 Nitro Crossing	25 The 2 Line Bridge
9 Wild Woozy	
10 Swinging Tires	
11 TP Shuffle	
12 The Maze	
13 Spider's Web	
14 Whale Watch	
15 Alligator Islands	
16 The King's Finger	
17 Giant king's Finger	

Farm & Wildlife Center

Ⓐ Wildlife Rehabilitation Center
Ⓑ Children's Farm
Ⓒ Cow Barn
Ⓓ Nature Center/Exotic Animals
Ⓓ Outdoor Education Offices
Ⓔ Greenhouse/Hunts Brook Farm
Ⓕ Horse Barn
Ⓖ Therapeutic Horse Riding Ring
Ⓗ Animal Memorial Garden

Camp Cuheca

Ⓘ Rose Lodge - Log Cabin
Ⓙ Pavilion
Ⓚ Camp Cuheca Upper Campsites
Ⓛ Camp Cuheca Lower Campsites

L THERAPY • WILDLIFE REHABILITATION   CONTACT 860.442.9454 x4270

otherwise be successful in a traditional camp setting. The map showcases the array of land and activity centers at the Rick McPherson Outdoor Education Center, where Camp Cuheca is based. For campers, The Fourth of July traditionally marks the start of each season. The map displays the outdoor education center as it exists.

Visitors and students at Waterford Country School invariably found their way down to the horse and mule corral to visit Ginger. The influence of Rick McPherson and his farm team seemed to guide visitors that way through all seasons. The words of the mentors were everlasting. They shared with visitors that horses were a treasure and that youngsters can learn much from their spirit and beauty. The youngsters loved their poise and free spirit and often commented on their intelligence and loyalty. Moreover, children were always drawn to them because of their gentle disposition and friendliness.

There is never a dull day at the WCS farm. Whether it be cows sticking their heads through an office window and being nosey (above) or Wilbur the pig being roused from a long afternoon nap and covered with hay (right), there's something for everyone to discover at WCS. The farm is home to domestic live-stock such as chickens, potbellied pigs, sheep, goats, Holstein cows, horses, mini horses, and a mini donkey, to name a few. Interaction with the school's therapeutic animals and the environment is an integral part of life at WCS. The school maintains that the great outdoors is not just educational but also full of adventurous opportunities for learning.

Hidden in the beautiful woodland campus on Lake Cuheca is a certified ropes-challenge course. Adventure awaits as highly trained facilitators lead groups (above) through team building activities inspiring group cohesion, a connection to nature, leadership, and personal development. WCS programs, businesses, sports teams, schools, and community groups that participate are encouraged to enhance communication, have fun, collaborate, problem solve, and support one another on climbing challenges (below). Participants agree that no one walks away from a day on the course the same person they were when they arrived.

Ryan Tierney passed away on November 3, 2018, three weeks before his 20th birthday. He made his home in North Stonington, Connecticut, but his second home was on the farm at Waterford Country School. Tierney fought a very difficult battle with cancer for more than a year. He graduated from the school and worked as a farm staffer. Tierney had a special gift with the animals, especially the misfits that needed special care and attention. He inspired both students and staff with his willingness to handle chores without fuss or complaint.

Waterford Country School hosted a celebration of Ryan Tierney's life at the Otto Graham Gymnasium a month after he died. Instead of flowers, Tierney's wish was to raise money to upgrade the school's older farm equipment. Earlier, the WCS community donated money in Ryan's name to purchase a much-needed tractor. The farm staff believes that a piece of Ryan remains on the farm, a memory that helps children during difficult and challenging times. Pictured above, a student practices driving the "Ryan Strong" 300 E John Deere tractor during farm class. Pictured below, the WCS staff show their support for Ryan Tierney and his family.

Five

ROOTS AND WINGS

The baton of leadership was handed down unexpectedly in 2021 when Bill Martin resigned as executive director and handed the lead duties over to Chris Lacey, who was serving as the school's assistant executive director. Chris became the school's chief executive officer and was joined by Emily Thomson as chief operations officer, and Stacy Lowry as chief financial officer. (It is noteworthy that official titles of top-ranking officials at WCS in 2021 were changed to align the school with most company managerial structures.) Pictured above from left to right are Brian Rolfe, director of buildings and grounds; Bill Martin; and Chris Lacey, reflecting on the completion of the new WCS Founders Park in spring 2021, one of many centennial anniversary projects celebrating strong roots and a bright future for WCS.

Chris Lacey joined the Waterford Country School staff in 1998 as a lead child-care worker in the shelter program. He quickly advanced and became a supervisor in the shelter program and then later assistant program director for the Safe Homes Program in 2003. In 2006, he was promoted to program director for foster care, which eventually grew to include all the community services the agency now offers. Chris served as the community services program director for adoption services, children's outpatient clinic, intensive family preservation, and the foster care program at the satellite facility in Norwich for 11 years before becoming the assistant executive director overseeing all the agency programs. In 2021, Lacey became the chief executive director of Waterford Country School after 22 years of service. He obtained a bachelor of arts degree in psychology from Eastern Connecticut State University and earned a master of science in human services from Springfield College.

For the tenures of both Bill Martin and Chris Lacey, the pandemic of 2020 (and the variants that followed) impacted the operation of Waterford Country School. Adjustments to school programming as well as adopting standard precautions such as wearing masks, self-quarantining, social distancing, and handwashing were put into effect. By the time the Chris Lacey tenure began, many community members began to glimpse a return to "normal," and an attitude of "mend and make do" beginning to prevail. For pet owners and those with a penchant for all things wild, an increasing urge to turn to animals for emotional support became a means for gratification and comfort. Visitors to WCS exemplified how the social support provided by farm animals might also encourage more social interactions with people, reducing feelings of isolation or loneliness. For WCS students, the concept of open-air education brought vibrancy and energy to the campus and built a demand for new programing. A new Quality Parenting Center program (QPC) at WCS opened doors in 2021. The primary purpose of QPC is to maintain the parent-child attachment, reduce a child's sense of abandonment, preserve their sense of belonging as part of a family and community, and maintain cultural connections. Visitation coaches facilitate permanency planning, promote timely reunification, and aid in the decision-making process to establish an alternative permanency plan for the child in out of home care using the visiting coach model.

In past years, the asphalt and grass playgrounds at WCS were adequate but lacking. Basketball, dodgeball, kickball, and tennis were the usual mainstays with plenty of sideline space for lounging and chatter. Basketball was clearly the most popular attraction, with the pick-up games highlighting rivalries among the players. But summer would always take its toll, the players no doubt forever remembering the sensation of their feet baking in their shoes, a whiff of tar, and the heat radiating off the black surface. But this would change when Founders Park opened in 2021, an outdoor recreational center built for all programs at Waterford Country School.

At a campus celebration on June 19, 2021, an overflow crowd showed up to witness the opening of Founders Park and the WCS Founders Park Project committee announced the completion of the newest campus addition with founding family members (above). Bill Martin, retired executive director and visionary for the Founders Park Project, spoke of the park's meaning and importance (below). In his words: "After my unplanned announcement that I would have to resign from Waterford Country School, there was one thing that I knew we had to do before I left. My announcement of resignation sparked a fundraising and construction campaign to build this park in 90 days. With the focus of Julianna and the development office, the incredible design and marketing skills of Elena French, the construction focus by Ted Olynciw, Kathy Teel, and especially Brian Rolfe and his staff, and the help of dozens of board members and staff, featuring the stars of our Facebook marketing videos, Ben Turner with his guests Winston the Duck and some goats, Kelly Walker, Anne Adams, and Casey Saunders, the project took off. . . . So many people came forward with so much generosity, that it was just incredible. It seemed like a miracle to be able to get so much, so quickly."

Founders Park was a dream come true for the children and teenagers of Waterford Country School. Now, the campus offered recreational access to a brand-new outdoor facility as well as a state-of-the-art gymnasium. Who could ask for more? Happiness prevailed among students utilizing Founders Park for all levels of basketball as well as other sports competition such as four square, kickball, and baseball. The board of trustees was pleased with this accomplishment. They viewed Founders Park as serving the outdoor recreational needs of its population, including those needs of its many recreational programs. Inspection of the premises revealed a colored paved surface for basketball, a backstop for baseball and kickball, a teen playground, decorative fencing, lighting, and several gathering areas for socializing and activities. This was destined to be the central hub of the Quaker Hill campus and WCS were envisioned to use it for celebration, socialization and play every day.

This centennial stroll up and down memory lane of WCS draws to a close with a look at a few of the major annual fundraisers sponsored by the school. Family Fun Day on the Farm is one of the most popular events at Waterford Country School. The WCS Farm is opened up for families to take a tour of the grounds of the Experiential Education Center from 10:00 a.m. to 3:00 p.m. Family Fun Day features a variety of free activities designed specifically for children and families, including hayrides (as seen above), simulated farm equipment experiences (below), pony rides, sing-a-longs, crafts, animal exhibits, wildlife and nature exhibits and much more. Family Fun Day is free for visitors of all ages.

For over a decade, the Bring Your Mojo "Mr. Six" Golf Tournament has raised generous donations in memory of Gary Saunders, a WCS founding family member. This tournament is located at Great Neck Country Club in Waterford, Connecticut. The WCS development team and Scott Gladstone from Wireless Zone have led and infused enthusiasm into the annual event for over a decade. The event includes a shotgun start, a variety of entertaining activities at every hole including animal interactions, and a steak-and-lobster reception on the patio following a great day of golf. The tee shirt inscription (above), "Mr. Six," refers to the nickname Gary Saunders had because of his passion for Piper PA 32 Cherokee Six airplanes, which he marketed at Coastal Airways.

A golfer takes a break from the green and interacts with WCS's Winston the goose.